Writing Makeovers 3-4

Improving Skills—Adding Style

Written by
Alaska Hults

Editor: Sheri Rous
Illustrator: Yvette Banek
Cover Illustrator: Rick Grayson
Designer: Corina Chien
Cover Designer: Corina Chien
Art Director: Tom Cochrane
Project Director: Carolea Williams

Table of Contents

Introduction

Are you tired of trying to get your students to use words other than *very, good,* and *fun* in their writing? Do they repeat the same words over and over again in each sentence they write? Help your students learn new writing skills and "jazz up" their writing using the tools featured in this comprehensive resource.

Use the thought-provoking activities in *Writing Makeovers 3–4* to introduce basic writing skills, and use the independent practice pages to reinforce and support these new skills. Each section focuses on an essential writing component and features a coordinating mini-chart with suggested vocabulary or writing strategies.

The activities and practice pages show students how to
- identify sentence fragments and revise them into complete sentences
- identify and correctly use nouns, pronouns, verbs, adjectives, and adverbs
- choose the appropriate spelling for homonyms based on a given meaning
- identify and correct misspelled words in their own writing
- recognize and correctly use punctuation
- determine when a word should be capitalized
- choose clear, specific vocabulary to express their ideas

Strong paragraph writing begins with strong sentence writing. Use the step-by-step approach featured in this resource to teach students the key elements of a sentence, and then provide plenty of opportunities for your writers to practice their new skills with activities for the whole class, small groups, pairs, and individuals.

Select the activities in *Writing Makeovers 3–4* that meet each student's needs. Less fluent students will benefit from working with a partner or completing the first few independent practice pages in a small group.

Using the activities in this resource, students will become more successful writers while gaining knowledge of what it takes to develop better writing skills.

How to Use This Book

The activities in this resource are divided into sections based on the writing concept being taught. Each section includes whole-class, small-group, partner, and independent practice pages. Follow these steps when beginning each section:

Step 1: Practice Pages

Familiarize yourself with the section's opening page, which includes the order in which the activities in the section should be completed and tips for having students complete the independent practice pages.

Step 2: Mini-Chart

Familiarize yourself with the section's mini-chart. Enlarge the chart onto a piece of chart paper, and display it in the classroom. Also, give students a copy of the mini-chart to keep at their desk or in a writing folder.

Step 3: Whole-Class Practice

Have students complete one or more whole-class activities. This will give you a tool for assessing prior knowledge. Have less fluent students repeat activities in a small-group setting.

Step 4: Small-Group Practice

Have students complete one or more small-group activities. Partner up less fluent students with advanced students.

Step 5: Independent Practice

The independent practice pages get progressively more challenging in each section. Assign practice pages to each student based on his or her ability level. Review the vocabulary on each page, model how to complete it, and check for understanding before having students work independently. Have less fluent students work with a partner.

Setting the Standards

The standards listed below provide an overview of the skills presented in this resource book.

Reading

Word Analysis, Fluency, and Systematic Vocabulary Development
- Decoding and word recognition
- Vocabulary and concept development

Reading Comprehension
- Comprehension and analysis of grade-level appropriate text

Writing

Writing Strategies
- Evaluation and revision

Writing Applications
- Genres and their characteristics

Written and Oral English-Language Conventions
- Sentence structure
- Grammar
- Punctuation
- Capitalization
- Spelling

Listening and Speaking Strategies
- Comprehension
- Organization and delivery of oral communication

Sentences

This section focuses on building complete sentences. It asks students to identify the part of the sentence that tells *who* or *what* and the part that tells *what is* or *what happens*.

Getting Started

- **Define**

 A sentence must have two parts.

 A sentence must name a person or thing—this is the subject.

 A sentence must tell what the person is or does—this is the predicate (action).

 A sentence must begin with a capital letter.

 A sentence must end with a punctuation mark.

 A telling sentence ends with a period.

 An asking sentence ends with a question mark.

 A sentence with strong emotion or a command ends with an exclamation point.

- **Introduce the Sentences Mini-Chart**

 Give each student a Sentences Mini-Chart (page 7). Review the chart with students. Clarify any confusion students may have about a complete sentence. Invite volunteers to think of a complete sentence and share it with the class.

Guided Learning

Have students complete the activities on pages 8–9 before assigning the independent practice pages. Check for understanding by circulating around the classroom during guided learning.

Independent Learning

- **Super Sentences (page 12):** Before having students complete the activity independently, write a few sentences on the chalkboard. Invite volunteers to circle the subject of each sentence and draw a box around the predicate of each sentence.
- **The Aztecs (page 13):** Have less fluent students work with a partner or in a small group. Check for understanding by leading a class discussion about the story.
- **A Soccer Game (page 14):** Brainstorm with students different advertisements they have heard on the radio or television. Ask students to complete the reproducible and think about what item is being advertised.
- **Is It Complete? (page 15):** Encourage students to expand their sentences beyond the words provided in the boxes.
- **Add the Words (page 16):** Consider having students correct a partner's paper since answers will vary.
- **No More Fragments (page 17):** Encourage students to write sentences that make sense for the passage.

Wrap-Up

Have students write a paragraph that describes a favorite animal. Ask them to reread their writing to check for complete sentences. Have students circle the subject and underline the predicate in three of their sentences.

Sentences Mini-Chart

A sentence must have two parts.

Example: | Joey | ran to the park. |

A sentence must name a person or thing. This is called the subject.

Example: | Joey |

A sentence must tell what the person or thing is or does. This is called the predicate (action).

Example: | ran to the park. |

A sentence must begin with a capital letter.

Example: |J|oey ran to the park.

A telling sentence ends with a period.

Example: Joey ran to the park|.|

An asking sentence ends with a question mark.

Example: Did Joey run to the park|?|

A sentence with strong emotion or a command ends with an exclamation point.

Example: This park is huge|!|

Solar Power Sentences

Objectives

Students will

- simply state the parts of a sentence
- identify a sentence and a fragment
- transform a fragment into a sentence

Materials

- ℚ Solar Power reproducible (page 10)
- ℚ overhead projector/ transparency
- ℚ chart paper

Copy the Solar Power reproducible onto an overhead transparency. Write *sentence, fragment, subject,* and *predicate* on a piece of chart paper, and display it. Write on the board *Ryan jumps far.* Tell students *A sentence must have two parts. A sentence must name a person or thing and must tell what the person or thing is or does.* Draw a box around *Ryan* and a box around *jumps far.* Ask students which sentence part names a person or thing (*Ryan*) and which tells what the person or thing is or does (*jumps far*). Tell students that the part of a sentence that names a person or thing is the subject and the part that tells what the person or thing is or does is the predicate. Point to the subject and predicate for the sentence *Ryan jumps far.* Display the Solar Power transparency. Read aloud each sentence, and ask the class to determine if the sentence is complete. Tell students that if the subject or predicate is missing, then it is a fragment. Record their answers as *S* (sentence) or *F* (fragment) on the line next to each sentence. To extend the activity, have students revise each fragment on the transparency to create a complete sentence. Then, have them draw a box around the subject and a box around the predicate of the sentence. Invite volunteers to share their sentences with the class. *(Students should identify 1, 4, 5, 7, 8,* and *10 as* **sentences** *and 2, 3, 6,* and *9 as* **fragments.***)*

| Ryan | jumps far. |

Which Is It?

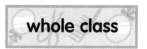
Choose a recent book that students read together in class. Write 8—10 sentences from the book on a piece of chart paper. Avoid sentences with a complex structure such as compound sentences. Display the chart. Have the class sit in pairs and silently read the first sentence. Invite students to confer with their partner to decide which portion of the sentence is the subject and which is the predicate. Invite a few volunteers to share their responses without commenting on whether or not they are correct. After you have heard from three to five pairs, circle the subject of the first sentence, and tell students *This is the subject.* Underline the predicate, and say *This is the predicate.* Repeat the activity with the remaining sentences.

Objective

Students will identify the subject and predicate of a complete sentence.

Materials

- children's book
- chart paper

Identifying Sentences

Divide the class into pairs, and give each pair a set of Sentence Cards. Have students cut apart the cards and place them in a pile faceup on their desk. Explain that some of the cards have a sentence and some have a sentence fragment. Remind students that they should look for both a subject and a predicate. Explain that even though each group of words begins with a capital letter and ends with a punctuation mark that it still might not be a complete sentence. If one part of the sentence is missing, then the card contains a fragment. Tell pairs to read each card and place the cards with a fragment in a pile faceup on the corner of their desk. Have pairs draw a circle around the subject and underline the predicate of each complete sentence. As pairs work, circulate through the class to check the fragment card piles to be sure that students have correctly identified all the complete sentences.

Objective

Students will identify the subject and predicate of a complete sentence.

Materials

- Sentence Cards (page 11)
- scissors

Solar Power

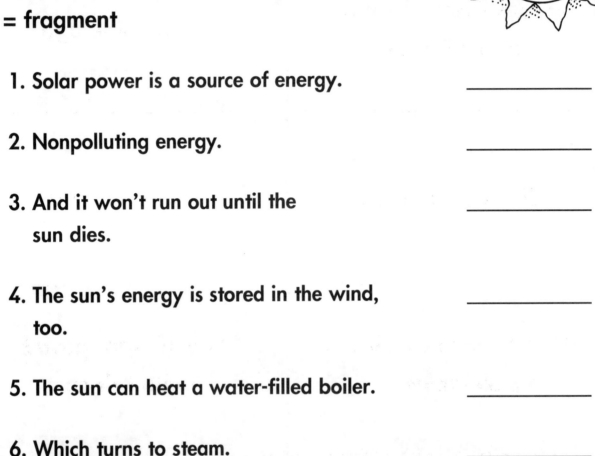

S = sentence

F = fragment

1. Solar power is a source of energy. _____

2. Nonpolluting energy. _____

3. And it won't run out until the
   sun dies. _____

4. The sun's energy is stored in the wind,
   too. _____

5. The sun can heat a water-filled boiler. _____

6. Which turns to steam. _____

7. Steam turns a turbine to make electricity. _____

8. California is home to some solar power
   plants. _____

9. Because it is a sunny place. _____

10. Space stations use solar power, too. _____

Sentence Cards

People lived on farms or in villages.	A long time ago.
Cities were busy.	Houses had no electricity.
Were lit with candles or oil lamps.	Streets were paved with bricks.
Dusty when dry and muddy when wet.	Animals, horses, and people.
People played stickball.	In the streets.

Super Sentences

Directions: A sentence has two parts. It has a subject that tells who or what and a predicate that tells what the person or thing is or does. Circle the subject in each sentence.
Underline the predicate in each sentence.

Children play soccer there.   I will go ice fishing.

You can play baseball, too.   He has a new bicycle.

She likes to dance.   Dan watches football.

They are on the hockey team.   You can buy hot dogs at
                                               the ball game.

Curling is an Olympic sport.   He is their mascot.

Writing Makeovers • 3–4 © 2003 Creative Teaching Press

The Aztecs

Directions: Read the story. Circle the subject in each sentence.

The Aztecs lived hundreds of years ago. This large group of people lived in South America. The Aztecs were ruled by an emperor, protected by warriors, and guided by priests.

They grew corn and cotton. They grew vegetables like tomatoes and avocados. They used cocoa beans to make a chocolate drink.

The Aztecs built large pyramids for their church. They invented a way to get water to flow uphill so that they could water their crops. The Aztecs were a clever and successful group of people.

Name _____   Date _____

A Soccer Game

Directions: Read the advertisement. Draw a line under the predicate in each sentence.

Parents, turn any area into a soccer field! Kids can use our portable soccer net anywhere. This net is blue with mesh sides. It comes with a built-in scorekeeper. The detachable target is great for practicing goal shots. The soccer net folds into its own tote bag. The soccer net is great for the beach or park! You can turn to page 12 for more information about our soccer net.

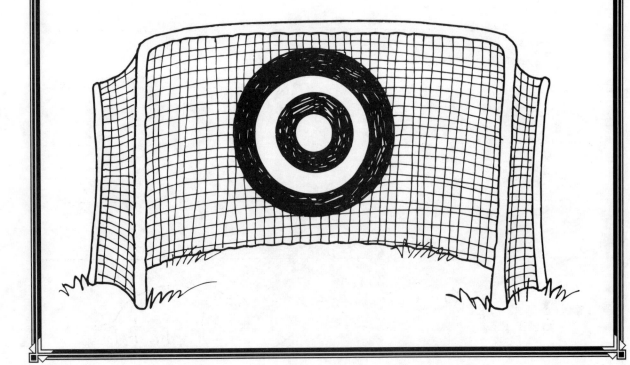

Is It Complete?

Directions: Combine the subjects and predicates to make five sentences. Add additional words not listed below to give your sentences more details and make them longer. Write your own original sentences on the last three lines.

Subjects	Predicates
Holly	is running
the store	does not grow on trees
John	is unlocked
money	yelled loudly
the car	drove quickly down the street

1. _____

2. _____

3. _____

4. _____

5. _____

6. _____

7. _____

8. _____

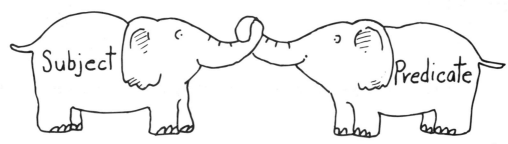

Name _____   Date _____

Add the Words

Directions: A sentence that is missing the subject or predicate is a fragment. Revise each fragment to create a complete sentence.

A star

_____

Our sun

_____

is very hot.

_____

Saturn

_____

is very far from Earth.

_____

can be seen by telescope.

_____

Writing Makeovers • 3–4 © 2003 Creative Teaching Press

No More Fragments

Directions: Find the four sentence fragments. Revise the fragments to create complete sentences.

Our sense of taste and smell warn us of harmful chemicals or rotten food. They are two of our five senses. Human beings can identify over 10,000 distinct odors. Less than some.

Only four. All the variations we taste come from combining these four kinds of flavors in different amounts. It is similar to combining primary colors to make orange or purple. The four flavors are sweet, bitter, salty, and sour. There is a part of the tongue designed to taste for each flavor.

Odors are made by tiny particles that float in the air. They are different shapes. Each shape triggers a different nerve inside of our nose. Sends a signal to our brain.

Smell and taste work together. They are connected by the nasal cavity in our head. If we can't smell. Food seems bland when we have a cold because we can't smell it.

1._____

2._____

3._____

4._____

Nouns and Pronouns

This section focuses on nouns that name people, places, things, and ideas. Students will learn to choose the correct pronoun to represent a given noun based on its meaning (e.g., *he* versus *it*) and usage (e.g., *him* versus *his*). They will also distinguish between common and proper nouns to determine when a noun needs to be capitalized.

Getting Started

- **Define**

  A noun is a word that names a person, place, thing, or idea.

  A pronoun is a word that takes the place of the name of a noun. Pronouns include *I, me, you, they,* and *it.*

- **Introduce the Nouns and Pronouns Mini-Chart**

  Give each student a Nouns and Pronouns Mini-Chart (page 19). Review the word lists, and clarify the meaning of any words with which students may be unfamiliar. This mini-chart lends itself well to pantomime. Invite students to take turns acting out the words on the chart.

Guided Learning

Have students complete the activities on pages 20–22 before assigning the independent practice pages. Check for understanding by circulating around the classroom during guided learning.

Independent Learning

- **Aunt Charlotte (page 25):** Encourage students to reread the sentences to make sure they have underlined all the nouns.
- **I and Me (page 26):** Remind students to use *I* as the subject of a sentence and *me* after action verbs and after prepositions such as *to, with, for,* and *at.* Explain that when you write about yourself and any other person, always name yourself last.
- **Moving Mountains (page 27):** Before having students complete the activity independently, invite volunteers to give examples of subject pronouns.
- **The Lesson (page 28):** Remind students that object pronouns follow action verbs and prepositions such as w*to, with, for,* and *at.*
- **Ours or Yours (page 29):** Students should draw an X over the following possessive pronouns: 1. *your* 2. *His* 3. *her* 4. *their* 5. *Our* 6. *Its* 7. *her* 8. *her* 9. *ours* 10. *its.*

Wrap-Up

Have students write a letter to a person in the future for a time capsule. Ask them to describe the people, places, and things that they have been exposed to such as inline skating, snowboarding, computers, e-mail, and cell phones.

Nouns and Pronouns Mini-Chart

A noun is a word that names a person, place, thing, or idea.

People	Places	Things	Ideas
firefighter	school	rug	honesty
nurse	work	book	truth
boy	store	car	kindness
girl	Utah	hat	
father	home	ball	

A pronoun is a word that takes the place of the name of a noun.

Subject Pronouns—tell whom or what the sentence is about.

People	Places	Things	Ideas
I	there	it	it
you	here	these	
he			
she			
we			
them			
they			

Object Pronouns—follow action verbs and words such as *to*, *with*, *for*, and *at*.

People	Things
me	it
you	these
him	
her	
us	
them	

Possessive Pronouns—show ownership.

People	Places or Things
my	its
your	these
her	
his	
our	
their	

Helpful Hints

✍ Use **I** as the subject of a sentence.

✍ Use **me** after action verbs and after prepositions such as *to*, *with*, *for*, and *at*.

✍ When you write about yourself and any other person, always name yourself last.

Person, Place, Thing, or Idea

Objective

Students will locate nouns and identify them as a person, place, thing, or idea.

Materials

- ♀ Person, Place, Thing, or Idea reproducible (page 23)
- ♀ overhead projector/ transparency
- ♀ index cards

Copy the Person, Place, Thing, or Idea reproducible onto an overhead transparency. Give each student four index cards. Have students write *person, place, thing,* and *idea* on separate cards. Tell them that nouns are words that name a person, place, thing, or idea. Write on the board *John and Julie get on the plane.* Ask students to find the word that names a thing. *(plane)* Tell students that *plane* is a noun and that every sentence has a noun. Ask them to find two other nouns in the sentence. *(John, Julie)* Point out that these words each name a person. Display the Person, Place, Thing or Idea transparency. Read aloud each sentence. Have volunteers identify the nouns in the sentence, and ask students to hold up the card that tells what each noun names. *(Students should identify the following nouns and cards: 1. **mountain**—thing, **Africa**—place, **Mt. Kilimanjaro**—place or thing 2. **pyramids**—thing, **pharaohs**—person 3. **animal**—thing, **land**—place or thing, **elephant**—thing 4. **elephant**—thing, **tons**—thing 5. **masks**—thing, **Benin**—place 6. **people**—person, **East Africa**—place, **nomads**—person 7. **runners**—person, **players**—person, **Africa**—place.)*

Replace It

Objective

Students will locate pronouns and identify them in a sentence as a person, place, thing, or idea.

Materials

- ♀ What Is It? reproducible (page 24)
- ♀ overhead projector/ transparency

Copy the What Is It? reproducible onto an overhead transparency. Tell students that pronouns are words that take the place of the name of a noun. Give examples of pronouns, such as *I, me, you, they,* and *it.* Ask volunteers to tell the class in complete sentences about one or two activities they participated in recently (e.g., *I went to the zoo. It was crowded.*). Record their sentences on the chalkboard. Then, have the class find the pronoun in each sentence. *I* will be used most often in student responses, so limit the number of examples. Display the What Is It? transparency, and read section A to the class. Use your finger to track the text so that students may read silently along with you. Discuss each question as a class, and record the answers. For section C, lead students to respond with *the listener* (or reader) and *the speaker* (or author) instead of a specific person's name.

Is It Common or Proper?

Copy onto the chalkboard the chart below. Tell students *A noun that names any person, place, thing, or idea is a common noun. A noun that names a particular person, place, or thing is a proper noun. All proper nouns start with a capital letter.* Divide the class into pairs, and have each pair copy the chart from the board. Ask students to complete the chart by writing specific examples of common nouns in the Common Nouns column and proper nouns in the Proper Nouns column. Point out that the proper noun Marie is a specific girl, the Southwest is a specific region of the United States, and Hot Wheels® cars are types of toy cars. After students have completed their chart, have pairs exchange papers to check their work.

Objective

Students will list common and proper nouns and distinguish between them.

Materials

✑ none

	Common Nouns	**Proper Nouns**
People	girl	Marie
Places	region	Southwest
Things	kitten	Hot Wheels® cars

Writing with I and Me

Objectives

Students will

- determine when to replace a noun with a pronoun
- determine whether to use *I* or *me*

Materials

✎ writing paper

Write the following sentences on the board:
David and I went to the baseball game.
Jane was calling me to the stage.
Anna, Beth, and I like to watch movies together.
Would you like to go running with me?

Read the sentences to the class. Invite a volunteer to underline the word *I* or *me* in each sentence. Tell the class *Use **I** as the subject of a sentence. Use **me** after action verbs and after prepositions such as **to**, **with**, **for**, and **at**. When you write about yourself and any other person, always name yourself last.* Divide the class into small groups. Invite each group to select a group recorder. Give each recorder a piece of writing paper. Have each group member dictate one sentence with the word *I* used correctly and one sentence with the word *me* used correctly. Have the group recorder record each student's response on the writing paper. Then, have each group choose one *I* sentence and one *me* sentence to share with the class. Write the responses on the board, and then check each sentence to be sure that students correctly used *I* and *me*.

David and <u>I</u> went to the baseball game.

Jane was calling <u>me</u> to the stage.

Anna, Beth, and <u>I</u> like to watch movies together.

Would you like to go running with <u>me</u>?

Person, Place, Thing, or Idea

1. The highest mountain in Africa is Mt. Kilimanjaro.

2. The pyramids were built for the pharaohs.

3. The largest animal to live on land is the African elephant.

4. The African elephant weighs about 4 tons.

5. Ivory masks can be found in Benin.

6. The Masai people of East Africa are nomads.

7. Some great runners and soccer players are from Africa.

What Is It?

A.

Jesse is an artist. She uses her computer to create artwork for the Internet. It is used on Web sites that sell items or provide services.

Who is **she**? _____ What is **it**? _____

Is **she** a person, place, thing, or idea? _____

Is **it** a person, place, thing, or idea? _____

B.

Abby and Kylie are sisters. They live in Rochester. Their favorite movie is *Aladdin, Prince of Thieves*. It is about a poor boy who finds a magic genie.

Who are **they**? _____ What is **it**? _____

Are **they** people, places, things, or ideas? _____

Is **it** a person, place, thing, or idea? _____

C.

You display a lot of patriotism. It is a good virtue to have. Will you help me hang this flag?

Who is **you**? _____ What is **it**? _____

Who is **me**? _____

Is **you** a person, place, thing, or idea? _____

Is **it** a person, place, thing, or idea? _____

Is **me** a person, place, thing, or idea? _____

Writing Makeovers • 3–4 © 2003 Creative Teaching Press

Name _____   Date _____

Aunt Charlotte

Directions: Underline the common noun(s), proper noun(s), and pronouns in each sentence. There may be more than one common or proper noun in a sentence. Try to underline all three nouns and/or pronouns in each sentence. Write each noun only once in the chart below. Remember to start each proper noun with a capital letter.

Example: <u>Aunt Charlotte</u> is a <u>nurse</u> at a <u>medical center</u>.

1. She is in charge of patients at the Lakefront Medical Center.

2. She has worked for the same doctor for five years.

3. She has a cat named Shadow.

4. Shadow likes to visit the dogs on Park Street.

5. On Shadow's favorite day she eats fish.

6. Aunt Charlotte and Shadow play games together.

Common Nouns	Proper Nouns
nurse medical center	Aunt Charlotte

I and Me

Directions: Use **I** as the subject of a sentence. Use **me** after action verbs and after prepositions such as **to, with, for,** and **at.** When you write about yourself and any other person, always name yourself last. Circle the correct phrase. The first one has been done for you.

April 17, 2003

Dear Mattie,

This weekend (me and Alex, (Alex and I)) worked in the garden. Alison helped (Alex and I, Alex and me) with the weeds. Alex talked to (Alison and me, Alison and I) about his trip to Italy. Alison and (I, me) were very interested.

Alex, Alison, and (I, me) went indoors to make lemonade. The phone rang. It was Karen calling (I, me) to see if she could come over, too.

Karen and (I, me) challenged Alex and Alison to a card game. We decided to play Go Fish. Alex was a very good player. He beat Karen, Alison, and (I, me) at the game of cards.

That was my weekend. (I, me) hope your weekend was good, too. (I, me) hope you write (I, me) soon.

Yours truly,

Linda

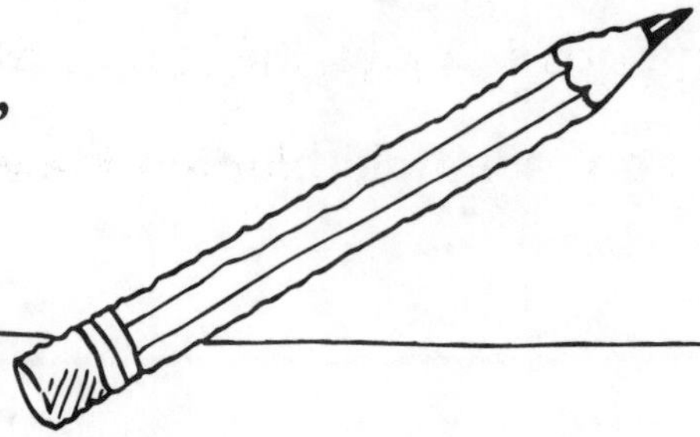

Name _____   Date _____

Moving Mountains

Directions: Subject pronouns tell whom or what the sentence is about. Read the Chinese fable. Review the nouns that are underlined. Replace these nouns by writing a subject pronoun from the box above each underlined word.

Subject Pronouns

Singular	Plural
I	you
you	we
he, she, it	they

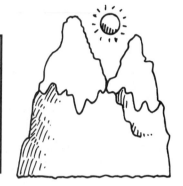

Long ago and far away, there was an old man named Yugong who lived near two rocky mountains in China. When people from his village wanted to leave the village, <u>the villagers</u> had to take a long, winding, and tiring route around the mountains. "If you and I could move these mountains, we could reach the south and the Han River easily," Yugong said. Everyone agreed, but no one knew how to move them.

Still, Yugong had made up his mind. <u>Yugong</u> took his many sons and grandsons, and <u>Yugong, his sons, and his grandsons</u> worked through the next four seasons, carving away small pieces of the mountain and carrying them away to the Bo Sea.

The king of the gods admired Yugong's determination, and <u>the king</u> asked two strong gods to move the rest of the mountains for him. From that day on, no mountain blocked the way to the south and the Han River.

The Lesson

Directions: Object pronouns follow action verbs and words such as **to, with, for,** and **at.** Read the story. Review the nouns that are underlined. Replace these nouns by writing an object pronoun from the box above each underlined word.

Object Pronouns

Singular	Plural
me	us
you	them
him, her, it	

Mike rides motorcycles every day. He knows a lot about <u>motorcycles</u>. So when Abby wanted to learn how to ride, she said to Mike, "Please teach <u>Abby</u> to ride motorcycles."

Mike said to Abby, "I will teach <u>Abby</u> how to start the motorcycle first." Mike showed Abby how to start <u>the motorcycle</u>. Next, he showed Abby the parts of the motorcycle. He pointed out the clutch, the throttle, and the brake. She pointed to the parts and named <u>the clutch, the throttle, and the brake</u>. Finally, Mike showed Abby how to start and ride the motorcycle. He handed <u>Abby</u> a helmet. She put <u>her helmet</u> on and rode the motorcycle.

Writing Makeovers • 3–4 © 2003 Creative Teaching Press

Ours or Yours

Directions: Possessive pronouns show ownership. Draw an X over the possessive pronoun in each sentence. Write a noun that could replace the pronoun in each sentence. The first one has been done for you.

Possessive Pronouns

Singular	Plural
my	our
your	ours
her, his, its	their

1. Is this ~~your~~ house?   _____Billy's_____

2. His picture was of the water tower.   _____

3. Will you throw her ball?   _____

4. This is their lunch.   _____

5. Our plane leaves on Friday.   _____

6. Its headlights are shining on them.   _____

7. Can you cut her hair?   _____

8. Throw her suitcase to him.   _____

9. This ball used to be ours, but now it's John's.   _____

10. It is running to its den.   _____

  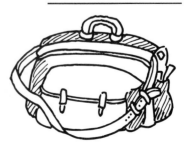

Writing Makeovers • 3–4 © 2003 Creative Teaching Press

Verbs

This section focuses on identifying verbs and replacing overused verbs. Encourage students to notice verbs that describe a specific action (e.g., *proceeded* versus *went*) when they read together as a class. Students who gain familiarity with new verbs are more likely to be comfortable with their meaning and spelling and less likely to depend on the same overused verbs (e.g., *said, went, come*) for their writing.

Getting Started

• **Define**

A verb is a word that shows an act, an occurrence, or a state of being. It may tell what someone or something is or was. A helping verb works with the main verb.

• **Introduce the Verbs Mini-Chart**

Give each student a Verbs Mini-Chart (page 31). Review the word lists, and clarify the meaning of any words with which students may be unfamiliar.

Guided Learning

Have students complete the activities on pages 32–33 before assigning the independent practice pages. Check for understanding by circulating around the classroom during guided learning.

Independent Learning

• **Jeremy McGrath, Motorcycle Racer (page 36):** Encourage students to skip the sentences they're not sure how to complete and come back to those when there are fewer words to choose from. Students should write, in order, *was, won, raised, earned,* and *raced* on the blank lines of the story.

• **Thank You (page 37):** Encourage students to review the words that show being before looking for them in the story.

• **Working in a Factory (page 38):** Check for understanding by leading a class discussion about the story. Then, have students find the verbs in the story. Review any challenging vocabulary such as *industry, economy,* and *constitutional amendment.*

• **Spider and Leopard (page 39):** Students might replace the overused verbs with words such as *roamed, spot, detect, gathering, hollered, remarked, called,* and *replied.*

• **Going to the Zoo (page 40):** The other two overused verbs students should find in the story are *gets* and *got.*

Wrap-Up

Have students write about a recent play or sports activity in which they participated. Then, encourage them to replace their overused verbs. Invite students to use the Verbs Mini-Chart for reference. Have them underline each verb they used. Divide the class into pairs, and have partners read their story to each other.

Verbs Mini-Chart

A verb is a word that shows an act, an occurrence, or a state of being. The following words are action verbs:

assist	frighten	look	support
deliver	grow	race	talk
earn	have	raise	think
employ	hide	run	thrill
enjoy	hope	shrink	use
feel	live	start	write

Am, is, are, was, and *were* are examples of verbs that tell what someone or something is or was. These verbs show being. They can also be used as helping verbs.

I **am** tired.
She **is** happy.
August days **are** hot.

He **was** here.
You **were** running fast.

Have, has, and *had* are examples of helping verbs that work with the main verb.

Carol **has** competed before.
Rob **had** won the prize once before.

Other helping verbs include these words:

be	could	may	should
been	did	might	will
being	do	must	would
can	does	shall	

This chart lists alternatives for five frequently overused verbs. Replace the overused verbs with more specific and interesting verbs.

go (went)	get (got)	see (saw)	make (made)	say (said)
advance	acquire	behold	assemble	claim
budge	allow	detect	build (built)	declare
continue	earn	discern	concoct	gossip
depart	gather	discover	construct	hiss
leave (left)	obtain	distinguish	create	holler
move	receive	note	devise	lecture
pass	retrieve	notice	erect	mention
proceed	win (won)	observe	form	remark
progress		perceive	invent	reply (replied)
stir		picture	manufacture	speak (spoke)
travel		regard	originate	tell (told)
		spot	produce	whisper
		visit	work	yell

Objective

Students will identify verbs in context.

Materials

❦ Rain Forest
   reproducible
   (page 34)
❦ Verbs Mini-Chart
   (page 31)
❦ overhead projector/
   transparency

Verb Hunt

Copy the Rain Forest reproducible onto an overhead transparency. Give each student a copy of the Verbs Mini-Chart to read. Discuss the definition of action verbs, verbs that show being, and helping verbs. Invite volunteers to contribute additional examples of each kind of verb. Display the Rain Forest transparency. Read aloud the story. Then read aloud each sentence, and have students find the verb(s) in it. Have them whisper the verb they found to a neighbor, and then invite volunteers to circle on the overhead transparency the verb they identified. To extend the lesson, ask volunteers to identify each verb as an action verb, a verb that shows being, or a helping verb.

pairs

Objective

Students will correctly use verbs in context.

Materials

❦ Verbs Mini-Chart
   (page 31)
❦ drawing paper
❦ crayons or markers

Word Illustrations

Divide the class into pairs. Give each pair a sheet of drawing paper and a copy of the Verbs Mini-Chart. Have partners fold the drawing paper in half. Point out that there are now four sections on the paper: two on the front and two on the back. Have students refer to their mini-chart and choose four verbs—one alternative for four of the five frequently overused verbs. Have students write a sentence that includes each verb at the bottom of a section of their paper and illustrate it. Combine the completed papers in a class book. On the cover, write each of the worn-out words inside of the international sign for "not" by drawing a circle around each word and a diagonal line through each circle.

Overused Verbs

Write the following sentences on the chalkboard:
1. He went to the cereal aisle.
2. He fled to the cereal aisle.
3. He proceeded to the cereal aisle.
4. He got money.
5. He earned money.
6. He won money.

Read aloud the first three sentences. Tell students that only one of these sentences tells what the reader meant to imply. Ask the class if there is any way to tell from the first sentence which of the other two sentences is correct. (No, *went* is not specific enough.) Explain that some words are overused and have only a very general meaning. Read aloud the last three sentences. Have students share which sentences give the reader specific information. Divide the class into small groups. Give each student an I'm Worn Out reproducible. Invite group members to work together to improve the "worn-out" verbs in the sentences by crossing them out and replacing them with more specific verbs. Then, discuss as a class which verbs could replace each overused verb. Have group members raise their hand when they hear a response they also chose. Discuss with the class why some answers were chosen more often than others.

Objective
Students will recognize overused verbs and replace them in context.

Materials
✂ I'm Worn Out reproducible (page 35)

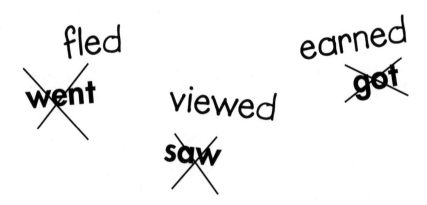

Rain Forest

Tropical rain forests of South America, Africa, and Southeast Asia are always warm and wet. Plants there grow all year. Rain forests are home to a large range of plant life. In turn, a wide range of animals and insects live well on the abundant food.

Most tropical rain forest animals live in the trees. They may travel along the woody vines or use tails, paws, or claws to move from branch to branch. They live off of the insects, flowers, and fruit of the rain forest. Birds, bats, snakes, and monkeys are some of the animals that live in the rain forest.

I'm Worn Out

Directions: Draw an X over the worn-out verb or verb phrase in each sentence. Replace these verbs with new verbs that give the reader more detail. Use your Verbs Mini-Chart for ideas.

Mary and Beth got a new baseball.   _____

Bobby is going to the park.   _____

We saw a new type of rock.   _____

She said she was hungry.   _____

They saw a girl on the street.   _____

Joshua went down the street.   _____

My dad sees a truck.   _____

The boy will make a new tree house to play in.   _____

Jeremy McGrath, Motorcycle Racer

Directions: Circle the verbs and helping verbs in the word bank. Use these verbs to fill in the blanks to complete the story.

Word Bank

earned	raced	smart
Jeremy	raised	was
quickly	red	won

Jeremy McGrath won more national championships of motocross than any other rider in history. He invented the freestyle motocross jump called the NacNac. As a young man, his goal _____ to ride in a stadium motocross race. He _____ race after race.

Jeremy was _____ in southern California by his mom and dad. He says that his father inspired him. He _____ his best grades in English.

Jeremy rode a BMX bicycle as a kid. He _____ his BMX bike from the age of 10 to 14. He was an expert rider. He raced up to 13 times in one week. By the time he was riding 250cc motocross motorcycles, he had the skills to be a winner.

Name _____   Date _____

Thank You

Directions: Read the story. Draw an X over the action verbs. See if you can find all 13.

May 8, 2003

Dear Aunt Caroline,

I am writing to thank you again for the plane ticket to Uncle Alex's wedding. I am grateful to you for such a thoughtful gift. I enjoyed myself very much.

I think the best part of the trip was the wedding itself. I used half a roll of film before they made it to the altar. I danced all night. I laughed when the groom shared a funny story about the bride. Then, I cheered when the bride and groom danced together. I hope to see you again soon!

Yours truly,

Megan

Working in a Factory

Directions: Read the story. Draw an X over all 20 verbs or verb phrases.

In the early 1900s, industry supported the American economy. Factories employed whole families. Many young children worked long hours for very little pay. Even children too young for kindergarten were working in factories and fields.

Children toiled six days a week for up to 13 hours a day. They earned as little as a few pennies a day. Factory owners knew they were breaking the law. They hid child workers out of sight. They ran child-labor inspectors off their property.

In 1938, Congress passed a constitutional amendment that set minimum wages for adults. As part of those changes, they made it against the law for children under the age of 16 to work in most industries. Children were now guaranteed the freedom to play and attend school.

Writing Makeovers • 3–4 © 2003 Creative Teaching Press

Spider and Leopard

Directions: Read the fable. Replace the overused verbs by writing an alternate verb above each underlined word. Use your Verbs Mini-Chart for ideas. Reread the story to check that your new verbs make sense in context.

One long winter, thick sheets of water fell from a dark sky and the people and animals were frightened. Unable to find food, night animals <u>went out</u> during the day, and still they were hungry. Finally, the rain ceased and the animals wandered out to look for food. That is how Spider met Leopard. Usually, Leopard wouldn't give Spider a passing glance, but this afternoon, even Spider looked tasty, so he stopped to chat and tried to look as if he might be friendly. Now Spider is thoughtless and naughty, but he is not stupid, and he knew Leopard was up to something. So he jumped behind a leaf and hid. Angry Leopard slashed about with his claws but couldn't <u>see</u> Spider. He went to Spider's house to hide and wait inside.

But clever Spider knew Leopard. So he spent the day <u>getting</u> food and visiting with friends, but finally, it was late and time to go home. He approached his house, humming all the while. "Hey there, my banana house! How odd!" <u>said</u> Spider loudly as he drew close. "My house always answers me when I call. Hey! Hey, banana house, I'm home! How are you?"

Deep inside the house, Leopard <u>said</u> with a small, high voice, "I'm fine, Spider! Come inside!" And Spider <u>said</u> with a laugh, "Now I know where you are Mr. Leopard!" and sprinted in a wink through the window and to the highest corner of the house. Leopard jumped and slashed at Spider, but Spider was safe and dry in the corner of the ceiling where he has lived happily since.

Going to the Zoo

Directions: The verbs **went, made,** and **saw** are overused in writing. Circle these verbs in the story. Replace these verbs by writing an alternate verb above each word you circled. Use your Verbs Mini-Chart for ideas. You may need to rewrite part of the sentence to properly use the new word. Can you find two additional overused verbs and replace them, too?

Yesterday our cousins visited, so we decided to take them someplace special. We made lunch and got in the car. We went to the zoo. At the zoo, we went in through the front gate. We saw two volunteers handing out maps. We decided to go see the pandas first. There were two pandas at the exhibit. They're on loan from China. The zoo gets to keep them for ten years and then they have to give them back. We waved at the pandas and then went to find the lions. The lions were roaring, so we said, "Roar!" back at them. There were three lions in the exhibit. One went over to a ball and started to bat it around. Another kept yawning. The third went back and forth by the water as if trying to decide whether or not to go in. We were running late, so we quickly went to the dolphin show. We were barely allowed in! The gates closed right after we got there. The dolphins made huge waves when they jumped. We saw four different kinds of dolphins.

All in all we had a great time at the zoo. We saw our favorite animals and got to spend a wonderful day with our cousins.

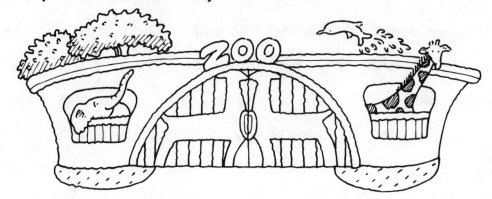

Writing Makeovers • 3–4 © 2003 Creative Teaching Press

Adjectives

This section focuses on the use of adjectives to develop meaning. Students will learn that adjectives tell *what kind* or *how many*.

Getting Started

• **Define**

An adjective is a word that describes a noun or pronoun such as a person, place, thing, or idea.

• **Introduce the Adjectives Mini-Chart**

Give each student an Adjectives Mini-Chart (page 42). Review the word lists, and clarify the meaning of any words with which students may be unfamiliar.

Guided Learning

Have students complete the activities on pages 43–46 before assigning the independent practice pages. Check for understanding by circulating around the classroom during guided learning.

Independent Learning

• **Suddenly Soft (page 49):** To extend the activity, have students write an ad for a new product. Challenge them to use as many adjectives as they can in their ad.
• **What Fun! (page 50):** Invite volunteers to read the words in the word bank to check for understanding.
• **The Jingle Dancer (page 51):** Students should also find the overused adjective *fun* in the story. Invite volunteers to read their revised story to the class.
• **Australia (page 52):** Model for students how to use the Adjectives Mini-Chart to select adjectives to replace the overused adjectives in the story. Students should find twelve overused adjectives.

Wrap-Up

Have students write a poem that includes at least five adjectives. Encourage them to choose a subject they know well, such as a sport they play or a hobby they have. Have students underline each adjective. Invite volunteers to read aloud their story. Encourage listeners to raise their hand each time they hear an adjective in the story.

Adjectives Mini-Chart

An adjective is a word that describes a noun or pronoun such as a person, place, thing, or idea.

An adjective tells . . .

WHAT KIND

Color	Size	Shape	Weather
coral	huge	boxy	clear
dusky	little	oval	foggy
pink	tiny	round	rainy
red	vast	square	windy

Taste	Look	Smell	Feel	Sound
sour	bent	fresh	bumpy	buzz
sweet	straight	salty	icy	coo
tart	tidy	stinky	slimy	purr

HOW MANY

fifty
many
several
two

Some adjectives are overused. Replace these words with less common adjectives that give your reader more information.

good	great	fun	nice	lots
acceptable	incredible	enjoyable	courteous	abundant
adequate	inspiring	exciting	friendly	countless
all right	magnificent	fantastic	kind	many
satisfactory	mighty	splendid	pleasant	numerous
fine	noble	wonderful	polite	plentiful

Writing Makeovers • 3–4 © 2003 Creative Teaching Press

Give Me a Description

Ask students to bring from home some common objects from their kitchen. (Remind them to leave anything with sharp edges at home.) Label each item with a piece of tape and the owner's name. Have a few volunteers sort the items into like groups (e.g., all the spatulas together). Display the groups of items on a table where students can easily see them. Tell the class you are thinking of one of the items. Ask them to indicate by a show of hands which item they think you have chosen. Record the votes on the board. Then, invite students to ask questions that help them determine which item you are thinking of. Record their questions on chart paper, and write each answer (e.g., *What color is the object?* white *Is the object big or little?* little *Is it light or heavy?* light *Could you use it to measure?* yes). After students identify the object, ask them how the questions helped them find the item. Elicit that the questions gave more information about the object. Explain that the color, shape, and size words are called adjectives. Hold up other objects from the table, and have students name color, shape, and size words to describe them. Record any new words on the chart paper. Read aloud the list with the class, and tell students that these color, shape, and size words can be used to describe people, places, and things (nouns).

Objective

Students will generate adjectives to describe the color, size, and shape of common kitchen objects.

Materials

- collection of common kitchen objects (e.g., measuring cups, plastic containers, wooden spoons, plastic cups)
- masking tape
- chart paper

Objective

Students will identify adjectives in context.

Materials

- Storm's Ahead! (page 47)
- overhead projector/ transparency

Describe It

Copy the Storm's Ahead! reproducible onto an overhead transparency. Ask a volunteer to describe the previous day's weather. Record on the board the student's response in complete sentences (e.g., *Yesterday was rainy. It was a cold and windy day.*). Invite volunteers to underline the nouns (i.e., *yesterday, day*). Tell students that the words that identify the day are nouns. Ask students to find the words that describe the day (i.e., *rainy, cold, windy*). Circle these words. Tell students the circled words tell what kind of day it was and are adjectives. Display the Storm's Ahead! transparency. Invite volunteers to read each sentence. Have the rest of the class read silently with the volunteer. Ask *What word or words in this sentence are nouns?* Underline the words that students identify as nouns. Ask *What word or words describe these nouns?* Circle the words students identify as descriptors. Tell students that some sentences may include more than one noun and adjective. For the first three sentences, model how to transfer the circled words to the first blank of _____ describes _____ and the underlined words to the second line. Then, have volunteers tell you how to complete the remaining blanks. *(Students should tell you that 1. **Heavy** describes **rain** 2. **Cooler** describes **air** 3. **Warm, humid** describes **air, cold** describes **front** 4. **favorable** describes **Conditions** 5. **torrential** describes **rain** 6. **Damaging** describes **wind gusts** 7. **Severe** describes **thunderstorms, unexpected** describes **tornadoes** 8. **loud** describes **warning.**)*

Diamante Poems

Copy the Diamante Poem reproducible onto an overhead transparency, and copy the reproducible for each small group of students. Explain to the class that the word *diamante* means "set with diamonds or other similar sparkling decoration." Tell the class a diamante poem is set, or written, in the shape of a diamond. Explain that the most common form of the diamante has seven lines, is written about two contrasting or opposite subjects, and makes a comparison between them by moving from one to the other. Brainstorm with the class different contrasting subjects such as *cat—dog* and *summer—winter*. Record student responses on the board. Display the Diamante Poem transparency, and read aloud the directions. Ask for a volunteer to select two contrasting subjects. Record the subjects on the first and last line. Follow the steps for completing the poem. Ask volunteers to select an appropriate word for each line. Read aloud the completed poem. Invite students to read along. Divide the class into groups of two to four students. Give each group a Diamante Poem reproducible. Explain that each group will select two contrasting subjects and follow the directions on the reproducible to complete the poem. Explain that each group member must contribute one adjective to the description. Invite groups to share their completed poem. Collect the poems, and bind them together to create a class book.

Objective
Students will use adjectives in context.

Materials
- Diamante Poem reproducible (page 48)
- overhead projector/ transparency
- bookbinding materials

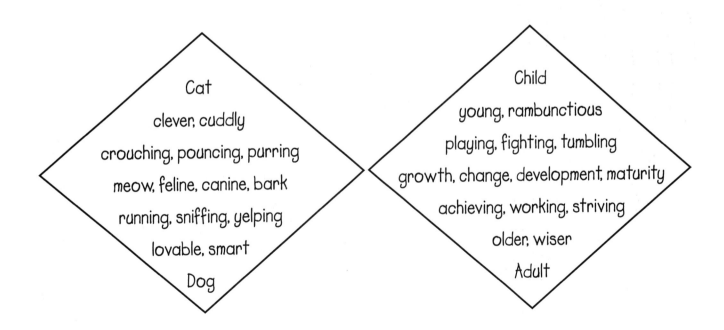

Cat
clever, cuddly
crouching, pouncing, purring
meow, feline, canine, bark
running, sniffing, yelping
lovable, smart
Dog

Child
young, rambunctious
playing, fighting, tumbling
growth, change, development, maturity
achieving, working, striving
older, wiser
Adult

More or Most

Objective

Students will use the adjectives *more* and *most* in context.

Materials

✎ none

Write on the chalkboard the word list shown below. Point out that many adjectives are used to compare two items. Explain that adding *-er* to an adjective implies the comparison of two items and adding *-est* implies the comparison of three or more items. Point out that longer adjectives use *more* or *most* in front of the adjective to do the same thing. Explain that students will pretend to brag about a recent accomplishment by using an adjective from the word list on the board. Divide the class into teams of three students. Explain that one player on the team will select an adjective from the board and use the word in a sentence. The next player will build on the preceding player's example by adding *-er* or *more* to the word and use it correctly in a sentence. The next player will add *-est* or *most* to the word and use it correctly in a sentence. See the examples below. Award a point for each word a team uses correctly. If a team uses a word incorrectly, play goes to the next team.

Word List

new	easy	common	difficult
old	tall	popular	successful
big	high	beautiful	obedient
tiny	warm	lovable	curious
few	long	wonderful	amusing
large	strong	independent	useful

Examples

graceful	long
I am a very graceful dancer.	I can run for a long time.
Soon, I will be more graceful.	I can run longer than Joey.
When I get bigger, I will be the most graceful dancer.	I can run the longest of all my friends.

Storm's Ahead!

1. Heavy rain is possible.   _____ describes _____

2. Cooler air will filter into the
   Great Lakes region.   _____ describes _____

3. Warm, humid air will   _____ _____ describes _____
   be lifted by the cold front   _____ describes _____

4. Conditions are favorable   _____ describes _____
   for thunderstorms.

5. Thunderstorms will include   _____ describes _____
   torrential rain and hail.

6. Damaging wind gusts past   _____ describes _____
   60 mph are possible.

7. Severe thunderstorms can   _____ describes _____
   produce unexpected tornadoes.   _____ describes _____

8. Take shelter if a loud   _____ describes _____
   warning is issued.

Diamante Poem

Directions: Write a diamante poem about a subject of your choice. Choose two contrasting or opposite nouns such as bat and ball. Use the following format:

First noun

Two adjectives that describe the first noun

Three verbs that tell what the first noun does. Use the *-ing* form

Two nouns associated with the first noun. Two nouns associated with the second noun

Three verbs that tell what the second noun does. Use the *-ing* form

Two adjectives that describe the second noun

Second noun

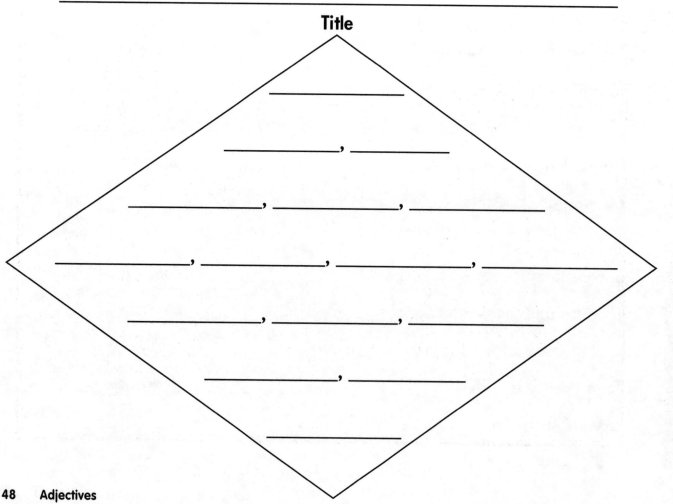

Title

Writing Makeovers • 3–4 © 2003 Creative Teaching Press

Suddenly Soft

Directions: Read the ad for fabric softener. Circle the adjectives. See if you can find all 12 adjectives.

Do you want silky, soft clothes? Then you need Suddenly Soft fabric softener! Add Suddenly Soft to your laundry for smooth shirts, soft blankets, satiny skirts, silky pants, and velvety towels. You will love the soft feel you get when you slip into your super silky, soft clothes. Hurry to your favorite store to purchase this wonderful fabric softener before supplies run out.

What Fun!

Directions: Fun is an overused adjective. Circle **fun** every time you read it in the story. Use the word bank to help you find alternate words and write a new adjective above each word you circled. Use each new adjective only once. Reread the story to be sure your new adjectives make sense in context.

Word Bank

enjoyable	hilarious	joyous	terrific
exciting	incredible	marvelous	wonderful
fantastic	interesting	splendid	

Friday was hot and Saturday was going to be hotter, so Mom said, "Pack up kids, we're going to Water World!" We all scrambled around gathering our suits and towels and fighting over the phone to call our friends to come along for a fun day. An hour later, there were eight of us crammed into my mom's van. It was so fun!

The trip to Water World takes over an hour, so on the way we tortured Mom with not-so-fun songs. It was fun to see her try to cover her ears at the stoplights. Then she started a game of twenty questions. It was fun to try to stump each other by thinking of really hard-to-guess answers.

Finally, we pulled into the water park. Everyone promised to remember where we parked the van and we headed inside. Water World has twenty-two different slides and four different pools. We made it our goal to go down each and every one of them. The twins were too young for the taller slides, but they promised to go down every one of the junior slides.

The Slippery Slope was the most fun! It is 200 feet high and has ten turns and fifteen drops! It was so fun. I told everyone else how fun it was and made it my personal goal to go down that one ten times.

Writing Makeovers • 3–4 © 2003 Creative Teaching Press

The Jingle Dancer

Directions: The adjectives **great, nice,** and **lots of** are overused in writing. Draw an X over these overused adjectives as you read the story. Use your Adjectives Mini-Chart to help you replace these words in the story. Write a new adjective above each overused word. You may need to rewrite part of the sentence to properly use the new word. Can you find another overused adjective and replace it, too?

Once there was a great shaman who had a nice daughter he loved dearly. She was terribly ill and he worried that he could not help her. He did lots of things to help, but still she did not get well. He began to worry that she would die.

That night he had a great dream. He saw a nice dress decorated with lots of shells. There was a single shell for each day of the year. A voice spoke and told him that if his daughter danced in such a great dress, she would recover.

When he awoke, the shaman made the dress he had seen in his vision. He asked his young daughter to dance in it. She did and was soon well again.

Today at every powwow in America you can find lots of jingle dancers in colorful costumes with metal cones that dance and chime as they repeat the fun dance. In one hand, they carry an eagle-feather fan while the other fan rests on their hip. They also carry the great hopes of their fathers in their hearts.

Writing Makeovers • 3–4 © 2003 Creative Teaching Press

Name _____   Date _____

Australia

Directions: Read the story. Underline the 12 overused adjectives. Use your Adjectives Mini-Chart to help you replace these words in the story. Write a new adjective above each underlined word. Reread the story to check that your new adjectives make sense in context.

Australia is a great place to live. It's also a nice place to visit! Last summer I went to stay with my aunt in Sydney, Australia, for two weeks. She is very nice and we had a great time.

Australia's nickname is Down Under because you have to go down under the equator to the southern hemisphere to find it. It is the fourth-largest country, but it is the smallest, flattest, and driest continent. It has six states and two territories.

The northern part of the country is quite close to the equator. It is hot all the time. There is a rainy and a dry season. The center of Australia is called the Outback and is the second-largest desert in the world. Southern Australia is cooler. While I was there, the weather was nice.

In Australia they speak English. It was good to be able to ask for the things I needed, but they use lots of words that we don't in America. Sometimes it was really confusing. It was fun to learn the new words though and use them on my mom.

Most of all, the Australians I met were super nice. They were great when I was lost and gave me lots of help. It was so much fun! I can't wait to go back again.

Australia

Writing Makeovers • 3–4 © 2003 Creative Teaching Press

Adverbs

This section focuses on the use of adverbs to develop meaning and add detail. It focuses on adverbs that modify verbs (e.g., *He jumped once.*) and that answer the questions *How? How Often? When?* and *Where?* This section does not address adverbs that modify adjectives (e.g., *His face was very red.*). Because the adverb is a more advanced concept than some of the previous concepts, there are fewer independent activities.

Getting Started

- **Define**

    An adverb is a word that tells *how, how often, when,* or *where.*

- **Introduce the Adverbs Mini-Chart**

    Give each student an Adverbs Mini-Chart (page 54). Review the word lists, and clarify the meaning of any words with which students may be unfamiliar.

Guided Learning

Have students complete the activities on pages 55–57 before assigning the independent practice pages. Check for understanding by circulating around the classroom during guided learning.

Independent Learning

- **Adverb Find (page 61):** Students should underline the adverbs *inside, every day, too, never, after, casually, soon, twice, happily,* and *sadly.*
- **Quickly Quench (page 62):** If students get stuck trying to decide whether a word is an adjective or an adverb, remind them that both types of words modify another word. Explain that adjectives modify nouns and adverbs modify verbs or adjectives.
- **A Very, Very Snowy Day (page 63):** Have students carefully read the directions. After students have completed the activity, have them read a recent piece of their own writing and replace *very.*

Wrap-Up

Have students write a friendly letter in which they describe a recent activity they participated in. Have students include at least five adverbs in their letter. Encourage them to use words from their Adverbs Mini-Chart. Ask students to reread their letter and make any needed corrections. Then, have them circle the adverbs. Collect the papers, and assess student understanding of the concept.

Adverbs Mini-Chart

An adverb is a word that tells *how, how often, when,* or *where.* An adverb answers the question . . .

How?	How Often?	When?	Where?
angrily	always	after	downtown
barely	frequently	already	everywhere
boastfully	never	before	here
casually	often	finally	inside
cheerfully	once	immediately	off
easily	regularly	now	outside
happily	seldom	since	southward
hard	twice	soon	there
loudly	yearly	then	upstairs
quickly			
sadly			
silently			
slowly			
swiftly			

An Overused Adverb

very	**Add additional overused**
replace with:	**adverbs from your writing**
awfully	
dreadfully	_____
enormously	_____
especially	
exceedingly	_____
exceptionally	_____
extremely	
fantastically	_____
horridly	_____
incredibly	
vastly	_____

Helpful Hint

✏ **Adjectives** modify nouns. **Adverbs** modify verbs or adjectives.

Writing Makeovers • 3–4 © 2003 Creative Teaching Press

My Collection

Copy the Collection reproducible onto an overhead transparency. Ask a volunteer to describe how he or she played a recent playground game. Record on the board the student's response in complete sentences (e.g., *I kicked the ball hard.*). Underline the verb (i.e., *kicked*). Tell students that adverbs give us details about an action verb or a verb of being. Explain that adverbs can come before or after the verb they describe. Ask students to find the word that describes the verb (i.e., *hard*). Circle this word. Tell students how the action occurred, and explain that this is an adverb. Display the Collection transparency. Invite volunteers to read each sentence. Have the rest of the class read silently with the volunteer. Ask *Which word is the verb in this sentence?* Underline the word that students identify as the verb. Ask *What word or words in this sentence tell **how, how often, when,** or **where?*** Circle the words students identify as descriptors. For the first three sentences, model how to transfer the circled words to the first blank of _____ *tells* _____. Write on the second line *how, how often, when,* or *where*. Then, have volunteers tell you how to complete the remaining blanks. *(Students should find 1. **passionately** tells **how** 2. **seldom** tells **how often** 3. **regularly** tells **how often** 4. **inside** tells **where** 5. **cheerfully** tells **how** 6. **everywhere** tells **where** 7. **frequently** tells **how often** 8. **happily** tells **how**.)*

Objectives

Students will
- identify verbs in sentences
- recognize that adverbs describe verbs

Materials

- Collection reproducible (page 58)
- overhead projector/ transparency

Too Many Very's

Objective

Students will replace *very* with less common adverbs.

Materials

- Very Common Word reproducible (page 59)
- overhead projector/ transparency

Copy the Very Common Word reproducible onto an overhead transparency. Write *He skates very well* and *That house is very red* on the board. Underline *skates* and *house*. Tell students that an adverb is a modifier because it modifies, or changes, the meaning of another word. Explain that an adverb can modify or change the meaning of a verb, but it can also modify or change the meaning of an adjective. Point to *skates*, and ask *How does he skate?* (very well) Explain that in this sentence *well* describes *skates*, so *well* is an adverb, but it is modified by the adverb *very* to imply that he skates unusually well. Next, point to *house*, and ask *What color is the house?* (red) Explain that in this sentence *red* describes *house*, so *red* is an adjective, but it is modified by the adverb *very* to imply that the house is especially red. Tell students that the adverb *very* tells the reader that an object or quality is more than usually expected. However, because *very* is so overused, readers tend to barely register the word as they are reading. Draw an X over *very* in the first sentence, and write *exceptionally*. Draw an X over *very* in the second sentence, and write *horridly*. Tell students that the meaning in the first sentence is the same but the new adverb is less common and calls more attention to the meaning. In the second sentence, *horridly* calls more attention to the meaning of the sentence than *very* and also offers more specific information. The house is not simply more red than usual, it is too red for decent taste. Display the Very Common Word transparency, and have students brainstorm words to replace *very* in each sentence. Rewrite each new sentence.

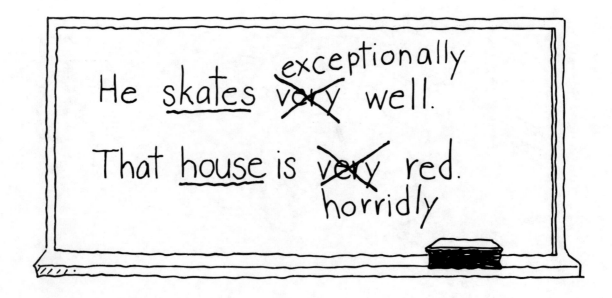

Adverb Sort

Copy the Adverb Cards onto an overhead transparency, and cut them apart. Copy a set of cards for each pair of students. Display the transparency cards. Read the words together, making sure that students understand the meaning of each word. Place the *How? How Often? When?* and *Where?* cards at the top of the overhead projector. Read a word card, and ask *What question does this word answer?* Invite a volunteer to place the word card underneath the correct heading. Continue the activity with a few more cards. Divide the class into pairs, and give each pair a set of Adverb Cards to cut apart. Have pairs lay the *How? How Often? When?* and *Where?* cards faceup. Tell pairs to shuffle the remaining word cards and then take turns flipping them over and deciding which question the card answers. Have them lay each card faceup below the corresponding question card. Circulate among pairs to offer suggestions as needed. After pairs have completed their word sort, repeat the activity as a class using the transparency cards. After you have sorted the cards together, read each column of words. Have pairs check their work by turning over the corresponding card after you read it—any cards left over when you have finished a column are in the incorrect category. Before ending the activity, remind students that words that tell *how, how often, when,* and *where* are adverbs.

pairs

Objectives

Students will

- review what types of words are adverbs
- sort adverbs according to the detail each word provides

Materials

- ✂ Adverb Cards (page 60)
- ✂ overhead projector/ transparency
- ✂ scissors

Where?	When?	How?	How Often?

	never		once

Collection

1. Chris collects mini
   bikes passionately.

   _____ tells _____

2. He seldom buys two
   of the same bike.

   _____ tells _____

3. He regularly rides his bikes.

   _____ tells _____

4. He keeps them inside the
   garage.

   _____ tells _____

5. On Saturdays, you hear him
   cheerfully cleaning the bikes.

   _____ tells _____

6. He rides the red bike
   everywhere.

   _____ tells _____

7. Chris frequently invites
   friends to ride with him.

   _____ tells _____

8. He happily races
   them at the track.

   _____ tells _____

Writing Makeovers • 3–4 © 2003 Creative Teaching Press

Very Common Word

1. It was a very hot day.

_____

2. Max eats very slowly.

_____

3. She writes very well.

_____

4. The sky is very cloudy.

_____

5. I am very sleepy.

_____

6. Pam is very smart.

_____

7. Ben swims very fast.

_____

8. Skippy barks very loudly.

_____

9. Milo climbs very high.

_____

10. That car is very green.

_____

Adverb Cards

Where?	When?	How?
How Often?	downtown	upstairs
angrily	never	frequently
silently	immediately	easily
inside	outside	soon
finally	often	loudly
sadly	once	seldom

Adverb Find

Directions: Underline the adverb in each sentence.

1. Put the gift inside this box and wrap it.

2. John eats lunch every day.

3. It is too hard to chew this rock candy.

4. Cory has cavities because he never brushes his teeth.

5. He washed his hands after he touched the bird.

6. He casually took off the lid.

7. Ally will eat lunch soon.

8. Abby honked the horn twice.

9. Darren happily fixed the bike.

10. Bonnie sadly closed the book.

Name _____   Date _____

Quickly Quench

Directions: Read the ad for Quickly Quench. Circle the eight adverbs. Be careful since there are plenty of adjectives in this ad, too. **Helpful Hint:** Adjectives modify nouns and adverbs modify verbs or adjectives.

Quickly Quench is the new sports drink from Sugary Enterprises. Ruthann runs quickly every day of the week. She easily runs past the other joggers. How does she do it? She drinks Quickly Quench before and after she runs!

Roger swiftly swims a mile before breakfast! He slowly sank in the water until he discovered Quickly Quench! Now he wins every race by rapidly racing to the finish line. Regularly drink Quickly Quench and you can, too!

 # A Very, Very Snow Day

Directions: The word **very** is overused in writing. Circle **very** every time you read it in the story. Use the word bank to help you find alternate adverbs. Write a different adverb above each word you circled. Reread the story to check that your new adverbs make sense in context.

Word Bank

awfully	extremely	marvelously	unusually
exceptionally	fantastically	quite	wonderfully
extraordinarily	incredibly	undeniably	

It was very cold. We looked outside and noticed that it was snowing very hard. We listened to the radio to see if we would have to go to school. At 6:30 a.m., they said the name of our school—Chapman Elementary has a snow day! My brother Chuck was very sleepy and went back to bed. The rest of us pulled on our snow pants, parkas, boots, mittens, hats, and scarves and headed out into the snow. The snow was very deep!

The snow was perfect. We made a fort so we could throw snowballs at Mr. Jacobs when he came to deliver the mail, but he was very late that morning, so we abandoned our post. We were very hungry, so we headed inside for breakfast. Our mom was very mad because we tracked snow into the kitchen, but she was very forgiving and made us pancakes for breakfast.

We spent most of the day sledding, drinking hot chocolate in the Hansen kitchen, and eating the goodies all the moms had sent over. It was a very special day. I wish it could be a snow day every day!

Spelling

This section focuses on how spelling affects the meaning of a passage. Students will see how poor spelling interferes with the reader's ability to understand the writer's message. Students will discriminate between correctly and incorrectly spelled words in context.

Getting Started
• **Introduce the Spelling Mini-Chart**
Give each student a Spelling Mini-Chart (page 65). Review the word lists, and clarify the meaning of any words with which students may be unfamiliar.

Guided Learning
Have students complete the activities on pages 66–67 before assigning the independent practice pages. Check for understanding by circulating around the classroom during guided learning.

Independent Learning
• **Find It, Fix It (page 70):** Students should locate and correct the words: 1. *were* 2. *always* 3. *really* 4. *said* 5. *sometimes* 6. *finally* 7. *That's* 8. *there* 9. *know* and 10. *different*.
• **Make the Right Choice (page 71):** If students do not immediately find the misspelled words, encourage them to look at each word and consider whether it is the correct spelling for the meaning in that context. Students should circle the following answers: 1. *d* 2. *c* 3. *a* 4. *c* 5. *d* 6. *d* 7. *a* 8. *b*.
• **Homophone Crossword (page 72):** Before having students complete this activity, review how to complete a crossword puzzle.
• **Zippin' Zoom (page 73):** This ad contains a combination of frequently misspelled words and improperly used homophones. Have students consider meaning when they look for misspelled words.
• **Football (page 74):** This reproducible focuses on frequently misspelled words.

Wrap-Up
Have students write a lost-and-found ad that describes a pet or beloved object. Remind them to include details that identify the pet or object. Have students reread their finished piece and check for correct punctuation.

Spelling Mini-Chart

Frequently Misspelled Words

a lot	heart	said	until
again	instead	school	upon
always	it's	sometimes	watch
because	know	straight	went
Christmas	only	team	were
different	our	that's	we're
favorite	outside	then	when
finally	personal	they	with
friend	really	trying	your

Homophones are words that sound alike but have different spellings and meanings.

aloud	knight	right
allowed	night	write
ate	meat	son
eight	meet	sun
by	one	tail
bye	won	tale
buy		
	pail	their
capital	pale	there
capitol		they're
	plain	
dear	plane	too
deer		to
	principal	two
its	principle	
it's		
	read	
knew	red	
new		

Objective

Students will demon-
strate a method of
remembering the
spelling of phonetically
irregular words.

Materials

✏ writing paper

Silly Spelling Sounds

Give each student a piece of paper. Ask students to write *people,
friends,* and *our* on their paper. Ask volunteers to contribute their
spellings to a list. Record on the chalkboard all the different ways—
correct and incorrect—that students spelled each word. When you
have a complete list, ask *Why couldn't we agree on the correct
spelling of these words?* (They don't follow a rule. You can't sound
them out.) Tell students that one way to remember the correct spelling
of an irregular word like *people* is to invent a silly pronunciation of
the word that helps them remember the correct spelling. Point to *people,* and say **People** *can be recalled by thinking of the nonsense word*
pee-oh-pul. *Whenever I want to write* **people,** *I slowly say to myself*
pee-oh-pul. *This helps me remember the* **O** *in* **people,** *which I normally
can't hear, no matter how slowly I sound out the word.* Ask students to
contribute a phonetic pronunciation of *friends* (possible answer: *fry-
ends* emphasizes the unheard *i*). Repeat the activity for commonly
misspelled words such as *again, because, finally,* and *until.*

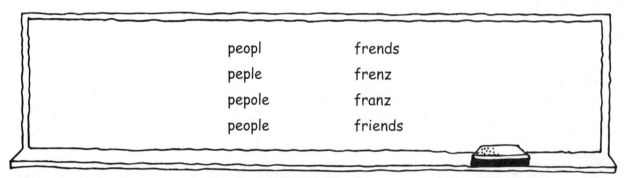

peopl	frends
peple	frenz
pepole	franz
people	friends

Objective

Students will discuss
how misspelled words
change or obscure the
intended meaning of a
phrase or sentence.

Materials

✏ Spelling Mini-Chart
(page 65)

✏ overhead projector/
transparency

Capitol or Capital?

Copy the Spelling Mini-Chart onto an overhead transparency, and display it. Highlight the words *capital* and *capitol.* Read aloud each
word. Ask students what the words have in common. (*they sound the
same*) Tell students that the meanings are different. Point to *capital,*
and tell students that it means *very important or the place where government gathers.* Tell students that *capitol* refers to the physical building where government meets. Tell students that words that sound the
same but are spelled differently and have different meanings are
called homophones. Explain that using the correct spelling of these
words is especially important so that the reader understands what the
writer is trying to say. Highlight *allowed* and *aloud.* Write on the
board *She is _____ to drive* and *She reads _____.* Ask for volunteers to correctly identify in which sentence each homophone makes
sense. Repeat the activity for two to four additional sets of homophones.

Word Search

Divide the class into pairs, and give each pair a Spelling Mini-Chart and a San Francisco Weather reproducible. Read the story once together as a class. Check student comprehension of the story with questions such as *Why wouldn't it snow in San Francisco?* and *What are two seasons they have in San Francisco?* Then, have each pair read the story again, find the eight misspelled words, and correct them. Remind students to check the mini-chart if there are words they are unsure of. *(Students should locate and correct the words* **Christmas, outside, until, again, said, always, school,** *and* **instead.***)*

Objective

Students will find and replace misspelled words in context.

Materials

- Spelling Mini-Chart (page 65)
- San Francisco Weather reproducible (page 68)

Homophone Riddles

Divide the class into pairs, and give each pair a set of Homophone Riddle Strips to cut apart. Have pairs shuffle their strips and place them facedown in a pile. Ask partners to take turns picking a strip. Tell students that each strip has two clues that identify a pair of homophones and the answers in parentheses. Solve one homophone riddle as a class. Say *The first word describes something you eat at a fast-food restaurant. The second word describes two people coming together.* Remind students that homophones are words that sound alike but have different spellings and different meanings. Invite students to discuss possible words for each of the clues until the class discovers that *meat* and *meet* solve the riddle. Then, have the first partner choose a strip and read it to his or her partner. If the student correctly solves the riddle and correctly spells the words, he or she keeps the strip. If the student cannot solve the riddle and spell the words, his or her partner returns the strip to the bottom of the pile. Play continues back and forth until students have solved all the riddles. To extend the activity, invite students to create their own homophone riddles.

Objective

Students will use meaning clues to identify a specific homophone and correctly spell homophones.

Materials

- Homophone Riddle Strips (page 69)
- scissors

The first word begins a friendly letter. The second word describes a wild animal. (dear, deer)

Names _____   Date _____

San Francisco Weather

Directions: Read the story. Draw an X over the eight misspelled words. Write the correct spelling above each crossed-out word.

We live near San Francisco, California, and there is no such

thing as a white Chrismas. You might need a jacket to go outsid in

December, but it's not cold enough for snow. It does rain a lot here

entil April or May when the dry season starts. Then it starts to rain

agin in September. My mom sed that it is alweys a good idea to

carry an umbrella when you go outside. Since it doesn't snow here,

our scool has outdoor halls. Sometimes I wish they were indoors

insted.

Writing Makeovers • 3–4 © 2003 Creative Teaching Press

Homophone Riddle Strips

The first word begins a friendly letter. The second word describes a wild animal. (dear, deer)

The first word refers to a soldier with armor. The second word describes the opposite of day. (knight, night)

The first word describes a boy in a family. The second word tells about something bright in the sky. (son, sun)

The first word describes an object with no decoration. The second word describes a flying vehicle. (plain, plane)

The first word describes something without much color. The second word describes an object you carry water in. (pale, pail)

The first word describes a fable. The second word describes a part of a dog. (tale, tail)

Find It, Fix It

Directions: Read each sentence. Circle the misspelled word. Correctly write each misspelled word on the line.

1. Wer going to Japan next month. _____

2. I olways eat my lunch at the table. _____

3. She was running rilly fast. _____

4. "Come on in, the water is great!" _____

    sed Nancy.

5. He sumtimes comes here to visit. _____

6. I finaly got to see Mt. Trumpet! _____

7. Thatts red and green. _____

8. Put it down over ther. _____

9. Do you kno if she's coming? _____

10. Chris likes a diffrent flavor. _____

Writing Makeovers • 3–4 © 2003 Creative Teaching Press

Make the Right Choice

Directions: Read each sentence. Draw an X over the misspelled word. Circle the word below each sentence that can replace the misspelled word and is spelled correctly.

1. **She bought a jacket becuse it was cold.**

   a   bot
   b. boght
   c. becuz
   d. because

2. **I took a picture of the captal building.**

   a. pichur
   b. pitcher
   c. capitol
   d. capital

3. **Thayre not going fishing.**

   a. They're
   b. Their
   c. gnot
   d. knot

4. **Weer reading that book.**

   a. Where
   b. Reeding
   c. We're
   d. Redding

5. **"I can help your friend," he sed.**

   a. frend
   b. sayed
   c. frened
   d. said

6. **I need to talk to the prinsiple today.**

   a. tok
   b. principul
   c. tolk
   d. principal

7. **Are you alowd to go with the teacher?**

   a. allowed
   b. wuth
   c. alowed
   d. wit

8. **What are you going to bie for Father's Day?**

   a. by
   b. buy
   c. father
   d. fahter

Homophone Crossword

Directions: Read each clue. Find the incorrectly used homophone in each sentence and write the word correctly in the puzzle.

Across
1. John spoke with the principle.
3. I gave this scarf two her.
4. I eight a big meal.
5. Are these too boxes for me?
7. She read the book allowed.
8. She is coming with us, to.
9. The tiger had a striped tale.
10. An octopus has ate legs.

Down
2. I toured the capital building.
4. I am not aloud to stay up late.
6. She lives in the nation's capitol.
9. The teacher read a tail about a cat to us.

Zippin' Zoom

Directions: Read the advertisement. Underline the misspelled words or incorrect homophones. Write the correct spelling above each word you underlined. You should find 14 words that need to be fixed.

Late to skool agin? You need the Zippin' Zoom persinol

transportation device. The Zippin' Zoom attaches to yor back

with two wide shoulder straps—just like your backpack! It's

jet propulsion technology brings getting to skool into the

space age. Ate tiny arrows give you complete directional

control so you can avoid any obstacles in yer path.

Their are five models of the Zippin' Zoom. You can bye it

with optional lights for night travel, a stereo system for

you're favrit tunes, and alot of rilly eye-catching colors.

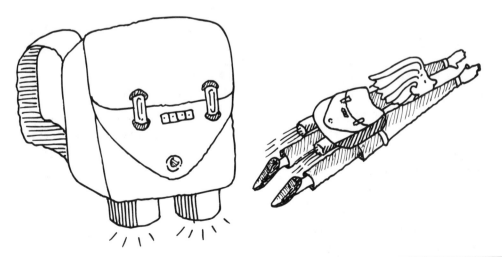

Football

Directions: Read the story. Draw a box around the ten misspelled words. Write the correct spelling above each word.

My friend is nuts about football. I don't rilly get it. I like the game. That is,

I like to wach the games with freinds or occasionally throw the ball around.

Even so, I don't know half the stuff he does about football.

He nos the names of every football team in the National Football League

and most of there star players. He doesn't just know their names. He knows

they're height and weight and a lot of little facts about how well they play the

game. I try to look interested when he tells me this stuff, but I admit that I

can't keep it all straight.

He has a wall of video tapes of every game he has ever taped on TV.

When he can't find an NFL game on TV, then he will watch one of the college

games insted. I think he knows the Ohio State University fight song. You might

think that's not a big deal, but we don't live in Ohio!

It will unly get wrse. He spends hours tring to get his baby brother to say

his first word, "football."

Capitalization and Punctuation

This section focuses on how punctuation affects the meaning of a passage. Students will see how a lack of punctuation interferes with the reader's ability to understand the writer's message. Students will identify missing punctuation and provide it.

Getting Started

- **Introduce the Capitalization and Punctuation Mini-Chart**

    Give each student a Capitalization and Punctuation Mini-Chart (page 76). Review the rules, and clarify any with which students may be unfamiliar.

Guided Learning

Have students complete the activities on pages 77–80 before assigning the independent practice pages. Check for understanding by circulating around the classroom during guided learning.

Independent Learning

- **Ladybugs (page 85):** Model how to draw an X over the words that need to be capitalized.
- **Benjamin Franklin (page 86):** Point out the use of a comma to separate the date from the year. Explain that the comma keeps the numbers from appearing to run together. Students should capitalize twelve words and add one comma and four periods to the story.
- **Chores (page 87):** In this activity, students revisit commas in a date. Remind them to also add any other missing punctuation and capitalize as needed. Students should capitalize eight words and add eight commas and three periods to the story.
- **Canoeing (page 88):** Encourage students to reread the story many times to make sure they have marked all needed capitals and punctuation marks. Students should capitalize eight words and add six periods, seven commas, one question mark, and four sets of quotation marks to the story.
- **Madeline's Birthday (page 89):** Students should capitalize thirteen words and add ten periods, seven commas, two question marks, one exclamation point, and nine sets of quotation marks to the story.
- **Paddle Wheel Boat (page 90):** Students should capitalize eleven words; make two words lowercase; and add five sets of quotation marks, one exclamation point, two question marks, seven periods, and seven commas.

Wrap-Up

Have students write an advertisement for an imaginary product. The ad should tell what it is, what it does, and why people should buy it. Have students carefully read their ad to check for complete sentences, correct punctuation and capitalization, correct spelling, and lots of details in the form of adjectives and adverbs.

Capitalization and Punctuation Mini-Chart

Capitalization ···

A word begins with a capital letter when it . . .

- **Is the first word of a sentence**
  How did you get in?

- **Is the pronoun "I"**
  I came in through the door.

- **Names a specific person or place**
  I asked **Nancy** to come in. She is from **Australia.**

- **Is a day of the week, a month of the year, or a holiday**
  The last **Monday** in **May** is **Memorial Day.**

- **Is the first word in a sentence that is a direct quote**
  Holly said, "**It** looks like it might snow."

- **Is a major word in the title of a book, an article, or a song**
  <u>Goodnight Moon</u>   "Rainfall"
  "Row, Row, Row Your Boat"

- **Represents a family relationship used as a proper name**
  Grandpa George but not *my grandfather*

Punctuation ···

- **A statement or command ends in a period.**
  The sky is blue.

- **A question ends in a question mark.**
  What color is the sky**?**

- **A sentence that shows strong emotion ends in an exclamation point.**
  Wow**!** The sky is so clear today**!**

- **A quotation mark is placed before and after the speaker's exact words.**
  "Wow! Look at that dog run!" hollered Alice.

- **Commas are used to separate items in a list.**
  Janet likes pizza**,** pancakes**,** and tacos.

- **A comma separates the day and year in a date.**
  January 1**,** 2003

Writing Makeovers • 3–4 © 2003 Creative Teaching Press

Dots and Caps

Write these sentences on the chalkboard:
john sees the boats from the pier
have you been to toledo
i will go to sleep
have you seen aunt Mary
the children wait in line
they play hide-and-seek with ben
Roger likes graham crackers He likes them with peanut butter

Give each student a copy of the Capitalization and Punctuation Mini-Chart. Have students read the rules and examples for capitalization and punctuation. Encourage them to carefully examine the examples. Have the class read each sentence from the board and suggest any needed corrections. Invite volunteers to make the corrections. Point out necessary corrections the class does not find.

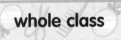
Objective
Students will demonstrate correct usage of periods and capital letters.

Materials
- Capitalization and Punctuation Mini-Chart (page 76)

> john sees the boats from the pier
> have you been to toledo
> i will go to sleep
> have you seen aunt Mary
> the children wait in line
> they play hide-and-seek with ben
> Roger likes graham crackers He likes them with peanut butter

Question and Exclaim

Copy the Question and Exclaim reproducible onto an overhead transparency, and display it. Tell students that question marks indicate that the sentence is asking for information and that exclamation points show strong emotion. Remind students that exclamation points are used at the end of an interjection or an exclamatory sentence. Choose volunteers from the class to add the correct punctuation to the transparency. Discuss the corrections students made in each sentence.

whole class

Objective
Students will demonstrate correct usage of question marks and exclamation points.

Materials
- Question and Exclaim reproducible (page 81)
- overhead projector/ transparency

small groups

Which Punctuation?

Objective

Students will use periods, capital letters, question marks, and exclamation points in context.

Materials

✂ index cards

✂ paper

Write the following information on separate cards. (If you have more than four groups, use duplicate instructions.)

Card 1: Write 3 statements or commands that are missing a period.

Card 2: Write 3 sentences without any capital letters.

Card 3: Write 3 questions that are missing a question mark.

Card 4: Write 3 exclamatory sentences that are missing an exclamation point.

Divide the class into groups of two to four students. Give each group an index card and a piece of paper. Have group members follow the directions on their card. Have groups trade papers, make any needed changes to correct the sentences, and then give the papers back to the original group for correction. Collect the papers to double-check students' work.

small groups

Race for Punctuation

Objective

Students will determine whether a set of words makes up a sentence.

Materials

✂ Punctuation Sentence Strips (page 82)

✂ scissors

Copy and cut apart a set of Punctuation Sentence Strips for each group of students. Divide the class into groups of two to three students. Have each group choose a team leader. Give each team leader a set of sentence strips to place facedown on the table. Have a volunteer in each group turn over one strip. Ask the volunteer to share if the sentence is correctly punctuated or not and if all needed words are capitalized. Have the group members evaluate whether the student answered correctly. Have groups mix up the strips and set them facedown after the student is finished. Invite group members to trade roles and repeat the activity until all students have had a turn. Then, invite group members to correct the punctuation on the incorrect sentence strips. Have volunteers share with the class what punctuation they used to fix each sentence.

Have you seen a good movie lately.

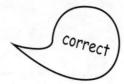

Maddy loves to play soccer with the other girls.

Commas in a Series

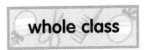

Write on separate index cards four to six sentences that require the use of commas in a series, but leave out the commas. For example, write *The children love the park zoo and circus.* Write on the board *Mary ordered tacos bean burritos and sodas.* Remind students that commas indicate a pause and that they are used in writing to make meaning clear. Explain that when the writer lists more than two nouns in a sentence, he or she must separate the nouns with a comma. Have a volunteer add commas after *tacos* and *burritos*. Randomly distribute the index cards to volunteers, and have them copy the corrected sentences on the chalkboard. Discuss with the class whether the changes made are correct or not.

Objective
Students will use commas in a series.

Materials
  ⚯ index cards

Who Is Talking?

Choose a piece of children's literature students have recently read. Write on separate pieces of butcher paper four to eight examples of speech from the book, but leave out the quotation marks. For example, write *This is exciting! shouted Bob.* For each example, prepare two index cards: one with the beginning quotation marks and the other with ending quotation marks. Tell the class that quotation marks are used to express spoken words. Explain that quotation marks come before the first spoken word and immediately following the last spoken word. Choose two students to hold each piece of butcher paper for the class to see. Give two students quotation mark index cards and paper clips, and have them attach the cards to the correct locations in the first sentence. Encourage the class to make any needed corrections. Repeat the activity with the remaining sentences.

Objective
Students will use quotation marks to express spoken words in context.

Materials
  ⚯ children's book
  ⚯ butcher paper
  ⚯ index cards
  ⚯ paper clips

Comma Puzzles

Objective

Students will demonstrate proper usage of commas in a series.

Materials

- Comma Puzzles (page 83)
- scissors
- resealable plastic bags
- writing paper

Copy and cut apart enough Comma Puzzles to make a sentence set for each small group of students, and place each set in a resealable plastic bag. Divide the class into groups of two to three students. Give each group a bag with a set of "puzzle pieces" and a piece of writing paper. Have group members use the puzzle pieces to form a correctly punctuated sentence that includes commas. As groups work, circulate through the class to check for accuracy. Once students have completed their puzzles, have them correctly write the sentences on their paper.

Place Them Correctly

Objective

Students will correctly place quotation marks in sentences.

Materials

- Use the Quotes reproducible (page 84)

Divide the class into pairs. Give each pair a Use the Quotes reproducible. Remind students that quotation marks show where spoken words begin and end in a sentence. Have pairs add quotation marks to each sentence. Invite pairs to share their answers with the class.

Question and Exclaim

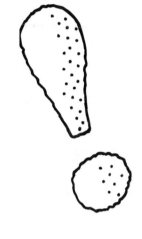

1. Hey_ Look _ There is an eagle_

2. Who is your favorite singer_

3. Ouch_ That bush has thorns_

4. When did Cornwallis surrender at Yorktown_

5. Do you have chores after school_

6. Yes_ Our team won_

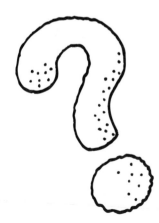

Punctuation Sentence Strips

The crazy cat jumped high in the sky.

Would you like some ice cream! Asked mom.

My favorite foods are strawberries, pizza, and popcorn.

Summer is my favorite season.

Have you seen a good movie lately.

Maddy loves to play soccer with the other girls.

"Wow!" said sally when she saw her new red car.

We took the train to Whistler, Canada.

We went to the island of jamaica last summer.

"It is over here!" Shouted Jamie.

Writing Makeovers • 3–4 © 2003 Creative Teaching Press

Comma Puzzles

Marybeth	likes	to	read	mystery
,	science	fiction	,	and
romance	novels	.	Charlie's	favorite
colors	are	magenta	,	green
,	purple	,	and	yellow
.	"	Wait	!	"
Joanne	said	.	"	Max
,	Maddie	,	Becca	,
and	I	want	to	go
with	you	.	"	On
our	vacation	we	visited	South
Dakota	,	North	Dakota	,
Wyoming	,	and	Montana	.

Use the Quotes

Directions: Add quotation marks to each sentence.

1. John said, Did you see that butterfly?

2. Hello, said Pam. I'm Judy's older sister.

3. Come and join us at the baseball game, said Corey.

4. Mrs. Oscar, said Ethan, will you please answer the phone?

5. We are here for the nature walk, said Ruthann, John, and Sarah.

6. That was an extremely entertaining baseball game, said Jacquie.

7. Pizza, cake, and strawberries are my favorite foods, said Tina.

8. Watch out! yelled Doug, as he saw the bicycle speed past him.

Writing Makeovers • 3–4 © 2003 Creative Teaching Press

Name _____   Date _____

Ladybugs

Directions: Add correct punctuation to each sentence. Draw an X over each word that needs a capital letter. Rewrite each sentence correctly at the bottom of the page.

1. today we are going to build a ladybug house__

2. "oh, good__" Jade said__ "Ladybugs are my favorite insect."

3. "can we paint it__" daniel asked.

4. "What color do you want to use__" asked mrs. Regan.

5. "Red is my favorite color__" said jeff__

6. the children attached the finished ladybug house to a fence post in the garden__

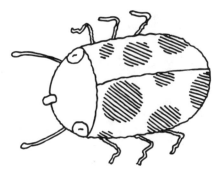

1. _____

2. _____

3. _____

4. _____

5. _____

6. _____

Benjamin Franklin

Directions: Read the paragraph. Circle each word that needs a capital letter. Rewrite the words correctly above the circled word. Add commas where needed. Add any other missing punctuation. Make sure each statement ends with a period.

benjamin franklin was born on

january 17 1706, in boston throughout

his life, benjamin did many things. he

was a printer. he formed one of the

first fire stations he also invented many

items, including swim fins. benjamin

franklin helped to write the Declaration

of Independence in 1776 he died in

1790 when he was 84 years old

Writing Makeovers • 3–4 © 2003 Creative Teaching Press

Chores

Directions: Commas are used to separate items in a list. For example, **I like dogs, cats, and tigers.** Commas also separate the day and year when writing dates, such as **January 1, 2001.** Read the paragraph. Add commas where needed. Add any other missing punctuation and capital letters.

saturday was declared work day at the jinkins' house That morning Dad assigned mike sarah and Miles to weed the flower beds. Mom was planting flowers vegetables and a cherry tree. Dad was mowing the lawn fertilizing the flowers and trimming the hedges By lunch, the work was all finished. We sat on the porch and had a great lunch mom made potato salad turkey sandwiches and chocolate chip cookies. that afternoon, the family played ball in the backyard. When the sun went down, we sat together and watched the movie toy story 2.

Name _____   Date _____

Canoeing

Directions: Read the paragraph. Use a **blue** marker to add the missing quotation marks. Remember that punctuation goes before the quotation mark. Use a **green** marker to add any missing punctuation. Use a **red** marker to add any needed capital letters.

Martha todd, alan and roxie were going to take canoe lessons at camp

They chatted as they walked down to the lake. have you ever been canoeing

before asked Todd. Once with my parents said martha It was a lot of fun I

just rode in the middle and they paddled. They got to the lake and met Joe,

who taught the canoe class First thing you have to do is put on the PFD's or

life jackets said joe. You never get into any boat without a PFD Then the

children were taught how to climb into the canoes and some simple ways to

paddle them. by the end of the first lesson, Martha todd Alan and Roxie

were able to paddle their canoes across the small lake

Writing Makeovers • 3–4 © 2003 Creative Teaching Press

Madeline's Birthday

Directions: Read the story. Circle the thirteen capitalization errors. Rewrite each word correctly above the circled word. Add any needed punctuation marks.

Good morning, madeline said Mom today is your birthday party Yippee

shouted Madeline is the sun shining Madeline quickly got dressed and rushed

downstairs she helped her mother clean up after breakfast put the toys away

and decorate for the party

The doorbell rang and Madeline rushed to answer it. hello, hunter she said

Please come in soon kelly Robin, max and Kevin arrived. The friends played

games and then sat at the table to eat hot dogs and potato chips Next, they had

cake and ice cream. Kelly said will you open my present first Madeline opened

Max's present and shrieked, It's just what I wanted finally, all the presents were

opened and the guests' parents were arriving to pick them up. Madeline said,

thank you, mommy. It was the best birthday party ever

Name _____   Date _____

Paddle Wheel Boat

Directions: Read the story. Circle the capitalization errors. Rewrite each word correctly above the circled word. Add any needed punctuation marks.

annabelle lucy and stacy were excited. today was the day Annabelle's mother was going to take them on a paddle wheel boat for afternoon tea The three girls put on their prettiest dresses with matching hats. Mom, do we look pretty Annabelle asked You will be the prettiest girls on the boat replied Mom. Come on! cried Lucy.

The girls climbed into the car and mom Drove to the docks there they saw the large paddle wheel boat. lots of people were dressed in their nicest clothes. Annabelle's mother led the girls up the stairs to a table on the upper deck of the boat. from there they could watch the paddle wheel Turn as they went up the river Look called Stacy can you see that eagle on the tree The girls gathered around and saw a bald eagle perched on a tree branch along the river's edge. As they went down the river, the girls saw a plantation house from the 1700s another eagle and some otters playing on the riverbank.

For tea they were served small pink cakes cucumber sandwiches and cookies. They all drank tea out of china cups. the girls chatted excitedly about their trip on the drive home, they decided that it had been the best afternoon of the summer

Writing Makeovers • 3–4 © 2003 Creative Teaching Press

Put It All Together

This section provides independent practice with the skills presented in the first seven sections. Students experience editing for spelling, punctuation, and sentence structure, as well as evaluating word choices.

Getting Started

- **Review the Mini-Charts**
  Use the mini-charts to review the previously taught concepts. Invite students to review the word lists and tips before they complete the activities in this section.

Independent Learning

- **Gravity (page 92):** Encourage students to first add any needed capital letters to the story. Then, have them circle the nouns and pronouns.
- **Dog Talk (page 93):** Have students complete this activity one step at a time.
- **The Seven Wonders of the World (page 94):** Point out that although *great* is an overused word and should be replaced in the story, students should not change *Great Pyramids* because it is the proper noun for the site.
- **Singing the Blues (page 95):** Point out that the final paragraph is one long run-on sentence. Students will need to determine how to break up the paragraph into clear, concise sentences.

Wrap-Up

Have students write an autobiographical essay. Encourage them to use the Editing Checklist (page 96) to carefully edit their writing for spelling, punctuation, sentence structure, and word choice.

Name _____   Date _____

Gravity

Directions: The writer of this story forgot to capitalize. Read the story. Cross out any lowercase letters that need to be capitalized and write the correction above the letter. Then find and circle the 22 common nouns. Circle each common noun only once. Underline the three proper nouns. Draw an X over the six pronouns.

gravity is the force that pulls any two objects together. gravity on earth pulls you toward the ground and gives you weight. in space, gravity affects the way planets and stars move.

isaac newton first described the law of gravity after he saw an apple fall from a tree. today we know that gravity holds together the ice and dust that make up saturn's rings. we know that the gravitational pull of the moon controls the tides on earth. we also know that gravity can exist between two large objects such as ships at sea or satellite dishes in space.

A person's weight depends on how much gravity there is and how much mass he or she has. a moose has more mass than a mouse, so it weighs more on earth. how- ever, if the moose is in space where there is no gravity and the mouse is on earth, the mouse will weigh more.

Name _____   Date _____

Dog Talk

Directions: Read the story. Draw a box around at least 35 nouns or pronouns. Correct any punctuation marks that are used incorrectly.

I'll bet you knew that dogs bark when they want attention, but did you know that they have other ways of talking to us, too. Dogs use the sounds they make and their body language to communicate to the people they live with?

Dogs tell us they want to play by crouching on their elbows. This move looks a little like a bow. Sometimes a dog will jump around from spot to spot, making little bows in front of you. This is a good time to throw a ball to it!

When a dog wants to tell you that it's angry or in charge, it will show all of its teeth. It will hold its tail all the way up and probably make a low growling noise. Don't try to pet the dog when it does this? Speak softly to the dog and slowly back away from it while still facing the dog.

On the other hand, a dog that wants to be your friend and please you may lie down and roll onto its back. The dog shows you its tummy to say, "You're the boss." Pay attention to the way that your dog behaves and you may learn a lot about your dog's thoughts and feelings!

Writing Makeovers • 3–4 © 2003 Creative Teaching Press

Name _____   Date _____

The Seven Wonders of the World

Directions: Read the story. Replace the overused adjectives *great*, *made*, and *nice* to enhance the story. Use your Adjectives Mini-Chart for ideas. Capitalize all proper nouns. Fix any incorrect punctuation and add any needed punctuation. Reread the story to check that all your changes make sense in context.

Have you ever heard of the Seven Wonders of the World? Did you wonder what they were or who decided they were great? The Seven Wonders of the World were the greatest buildings or monuments that the ancient greeks knew about.

The first Wonder is the great pyramids at giza in egypt. The pyramids are still great? We don't know exactly how they were made without heavy construction equipment and modern technology.

The second Wonder is the Mausoleum of Halicarnassus in Egypt. It was built by king mausolus' widow and is so pretty that today nice tombs are called mausoleums.

The third Wonder. is the hanging gardens of babylon. These great gardens are gone today but they were built by a loving husband for his homesick wife. They had lots of plants from her home kingdom of Media.

The fourth, fifth, and sixth Wonders are the Temple at Ephesus, the statue of zeus at olympia, and the Colossus of Rhodes. They are really good examples of ancient Greek architecture and art, but the Colossus no longer exists.

The final Wonder is the Pharos. The pharos is a great lighthouse that helped ships arrive safely to the harbor of Alexandria in egypt. It is in ruins now, but it does still exist.

The Mausoleum of Halicarnassus

The Statue of Zeus at Olympia

Writing Makeovers • 3–4 © 2003 Creative Teaching Press

Singing the Blues

Directions: Read the story. Capitalize the proper nouns. Underline any incomplete sentences and rewrite them above. Draw a box around four adjectives. Reread the story to check that all your changes make sense in context.

The american music tradition is filled. With variety. From pop to jazz to hip-hop, you can find a wealth of music to like or dislike. One of these musical traditions is known as the blues. and has been a part of American history for over one hundred years.

The blues first appeared sometime during the 1890s. It was around this time that ragtime and jazz were born also. Slavery had ended. And although most blacks at the time still lived in conditions that were not greatly improved from decades before, a great burst of creativity was the immediate result of this freedom.

Blues songs are based on a series of patterns made by musical chords. horns, such as the trumpet, guitars, and harmonicas are especially suited to blues music.

Today, the blues influences many modern artists, Jazz, rock, R & B, and gospel are among the genres that have blues roots, famous musicians like Eric clapton attribute their music to interest in the blues revival in the late 1960s, you may have heard the blues without even realizing it!

Editing Checklist

My writing is about _____.

____ I used a capital letter at the start
of each sentence.

____ Each sentence has a naming part (noun)
and telling part (verb).

____ Each telling sentence ends with a period.

____ Each asking sentence ends with a question mark.

____ Each sentence that shows strong emotion ends with an
exclamation point.

____ My writing has adjectives (words that describe the nouns).

____ My writing has some adverbs (words that tell *how, how much,
when* and *where*).

____ I checked the spelling of each word.

____ I wrote my name and the date at the top of my paper.

Writing Makeovers • 3–4 © 2003 Creative Teaching Press